ANIMALS THEN AND NOW

Steve Wilson

Contents

Rigby®

A Harcourt Achieve Imprint

www.Rigby.com

1-800-531-5015

Eras of the Earth

Many scientists believe the earth has been around for millions of years. During that time, the earth and the animals that live on it have changed greatly. Some of these **prehistoric** animals were not like any animals that currently exist. Others look like versions of the animals we know today.

The earth's temperature, **geography**, and atmosphere have changed. Some of the prehistoric animal species were able to adapt to these changes; however, many died out, or became **extinct**.

Scientists who study prehistoric animals divide the earth's long history into periods of time called eras, which are based on changes in the earth. The first era is called the Precambrian (pree-caym-bree-uhn), and it lasted from the beginning of the earth until 542 million years ago. The only animals that lived then were bacteria. Scientists think that the earth's atmosphere had very little oxygen. They also think that the oceans were olive green!

Bacteria are the oldest animals on the earth!

The second era is called the Paleozoic (pay-lee-oh-zoh-ik). It lasted from the end of the Precambrian until 251 million years ago. During this time, the earth had many small continents that eventually gathered together into one large continent called Pangaea (pan-gee-uh). Fish and reptiles first appeared on the earth during this era.

At the end of the Paleozoic, changes to the earth caused ninety percent of the animals that lived in the water and seventy percent of the animals that lived on land to die out.

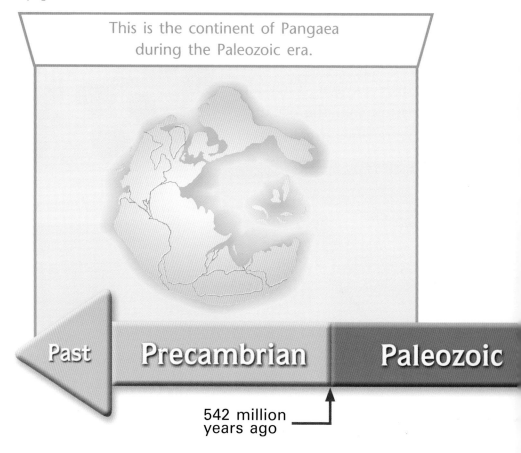

This is the continent of Pangaea during the Paleozoic era.

Past Precambrian Paleozoic

542 million years ago

The third era is called the Mesozoic (meh-soh-zoh-ik). It lasted from the end of the Paleozoic until 66 million years ago. This was the era of dinosaurs and enormous reptiles. Birds and **mammals** first appeared during this era as well. At the end of this era, dinosaurs became extinct.

The fourth era is called the Cenozoic (sen-oh-zoh-ik). This is the era we are currently in. Humans, modern animals, and modern birds first appeared during this era.

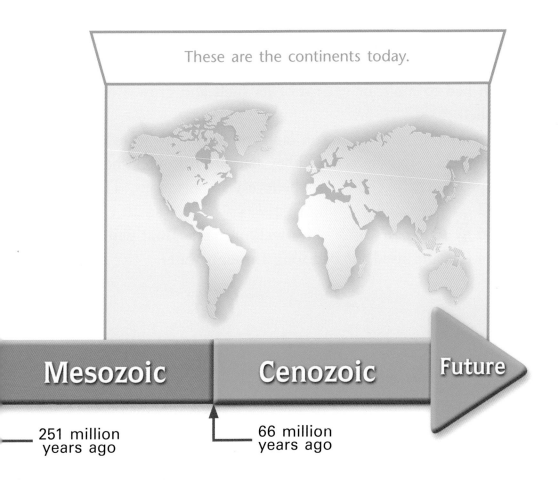

These are the continents today.

Mesozoic   Cenozoic   Future

251 million
years ago

66 million
years ago

Animals in the Past and Present

Sea Scorpions

Sea scorpions lived during the Paleozoic era. Most sea scorpions only grew to about eight inches, but one species could reach up to eight feet. This species was the largest known **arthropod** to ever live. In order to grow larger, a sea scorpion had to molt, or get rid of its shell and grow a new, larger shell.

Sea scorpions rarely went on land, preferring to walk or swim in warm, shallow water. They had a hard outer shell and a spiked tail that scientists believe was poisonous. They also had six pairs of legs. The first was a pair of small claws, followed by four pairs of legs for walking. The final pair of legs was flat and used for paddling through water.

This sea scorpion has used its claws to capture its next meal.

Horseshoe Crab

Horseshoe crabs are arthropods that also lived during the Paleozoic. While sea scorpions died out, however, horseshoe crabs **survived** and live to this day.

The horseshoe crab shares many of the same body parts as its sea scorpion cousin. Like the sea scorpion, the horseshoe crab has a spiked tail and six pairs of legs. However, all twelve of the horseshoe crab's legs end in small claws, and none of its legs are used for paddling. The horseshoe crab's legs surround its mouth, which is located in the middle of the top part of its body.

Horseshoe crabs can grow to up to two feet in length and live in warm, shallow seawater in the Gulf of Mexico and off the Atlantic coast of the United States.

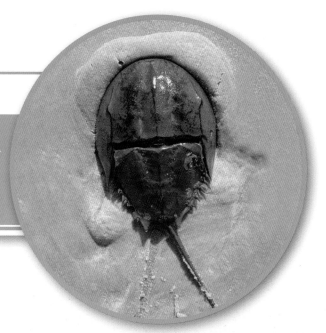

DID YOU KNOW?

The horseshoe crab is more closely related to the spider and the scorpion than it is to the crab.

This is the underside of a horseshoe crab.

Ammonites

Ammonites (am-oh-nites) lived during the Paleozoic and Mesozoic. They were protected by a hard shell. Some species could grow up to nine feet across! Most ammonite species, however, grew to less than nine inches.

Ammonites probably lived at the surface of the ancient seas instead of at the sea bottom. Most species of ammonite had flattened shells that helped them to swim better.

Many **fossils** of ammonites have been found throughout the years. The ancient Greeks may have used the round, flat fossils of ammonites in their Olympic games, throwing them long distances!

DID YOU KNOW?

This is an ammonite fossil. Some fossils that have been found have teeth marks from attacking animals.

Giant Squid

The giant squid earns its name by growing up to forty-four feet in length! It lives in very deep water and has rarely been seen alive. It may seem odd to think that ammonites are related to giant squid, but both belong to a group of animals called **mollusks**.

The giant squid has enormous eyes that are the size of basketballs. Its body is long and narrow, with a beak, or mouth, at one end. The beak is surrounded by ten long arms. Two of the squid's arms are tentacles that help the squid to catch its food as it swims by. The other eight arms are covered with suction cups to help the squid hold onto its food. These suction cups are also ringed with small teeth!

The giant squid was once considered to be a myth.

11

Meganeura

Scientists think meganeura (meg-uh-ner-uh), which lived during the Mesozoic, was probably the largest insect to ever exist on the earth. This early dragonfly had a **wingspan** of two and one half feet! It had two long front wings and two shorter back wings that could move independently of each other. This allowed meganeura to move in any direction and fly in place with ease.

Meganeura used these flying skills and its big eyes to spot its prey, which it grabbed in its prickly legs and ate with strong jaws. It preferred to eat other insects and **amphibians**. It lived in the swamps of what would become Europe and North America.

Some scientists think meganeura and other insects were able to grow so large during the Mesozoic because the atmosphere then had much more oxygen in it. Because of the way insects breath, more oxygen meant their bodies worked more **efficiently**, allowing them to grow much larger.

Meganeura would not be able to survive in the modern day because of the lower levels of oxygen.

Dragonfly

Today's dragonflies look a lot like their giant ancestors: they have the same slim bodies, heavy jaws, and large eyes. They are much smaller, though. The largest species of today's dragonfly has a wingspan of only seven and a half inches. One dragonfly species has a wingspan of less than an inch!

A dragonfly's wings have more veins in them than the meganeura's wings did, which makes the dragonfly's wings stronger. Their wings have other features as well that help them move more quickly through the air. Dragonflies are able to reach speeds of over fifty miles an hour, making them the world's fastest insects.

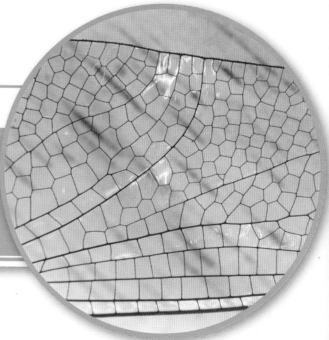

DID YOU KNOW?

This is what a dragonfly's wing looks like. The dragonfly's wings allow it to travel up to 85 miles in one day.

The dragonfly is usually found around lakes and streams.

Archelon

Archelon (ar-kuh-lon) lived during the Mesozoic. It was an enormous turtle that lived in the water. It grew up to thirteen feet in length, or the size of a van! Also, like some modern-day turtles, Archelon could live to be one hundred years old.

Archelon ate fish, jellyfish, and plants from the surface of the water. Archelon had large paddle-shaped flippers it used to swim around. It moved slowly, and it couldn't pull its head or flippers into its shell. This meant that despite its size, it was an easy meal for larger animals, which may have led to its becoming extinct.

Archelon weighed more than 4,500 pounds.

Leatherback Turtle

The Leatherback turtle has much larger flippers than those of other turtles.

The Leatherback turtle is the largest living turtle on the earth today, though it is not as large as its relative, archelon. Found in warm ocean waters, the Leatherback turtle can grow up to six and one half feet long. The Leatherback has enormous front flippers—those of adults can span over eight feet. Unlike other modern turtles, the Leatherback does not have an outer shell. It has a bunch of bony plates on its back that are covered with rubbery skin, which gives the Leatherback its name.

The Leatherback turtle has been listed as being **endangered** since 1970. This means there are not many left, so it is against the law to hurt or kill a Leatherback turtle. Groups worldwide are working to save the Leatherback turtle from becoming extinct.

Gastornis

Gastornis, a small-winged bird that lived during the Cenozoic era, never got to experience the joy of flying. However, its powerful legs may have given it the thrill of the chase, if only in short sprints.

The wings of Gastornis were too small to allow it to fly.

Gastornis had a very strong beak.

This giant animal could grow to a height of six and half feet and lived in heavily forested areas. Scientists who believe that Gastornis was a **carnivore** think the animal moved quietly to sneak up on its prey, as the trees would make it difficult for such a large animal to chase a smaller one.

These same scientists believe Gastornis used its massive beak to feed on tiny horses and other small mammals. Other scientists believe the bird was an **herbivore** that used its beak to crack nuts and attract mates.

Moorhen

The moorhen is brown, black, and white, with a bright red bill and yellow legs. It is much smaller than its ancient ancestor, Gastornis. The moorhen grows to only about thirteen inches in length.

Unlike Gastornis, the moorhen is able to fly, although it rarely does. It prefers to swim, bobbing its head as it moves through the water. The moorhen lives in marshes and ponds, eating mainly seeds and snails. It has long toes that let it walk easily on mud and floating plants.

Although the moorhen doesn't fly very often, when it does it is able to cover long distances. One species of moorhen migrates more than twelve hundred miles, flying only at night. The moorhen is found on every continent except Australia and Antarctica.

DID YOU KNOW?

These moorhens are fighting each other. During the breeding season, moorhens may battle over territory.

The moorhen has strong legs.

Basilosaurus

Basilosaurus (buh-sil-oh-sor-us) first appeared during the Cenozoic. Basilosaurus was an early whale that grew to an average of sixty feet long, although some could be eighty feet long!

Basilosaurus had good eyes and ears that it used for hunting. Compared to its body, its head was tiny, with forty-four teeth. The teeth in front were shaped like cones to hold onto animals like squid and fish. The teeth in back were shaped like triangles, for cutting.

Like modern whales, Basilosaurus breathed air. It couldn't stay underwater for too long. It would have had to come up to the surface in order to lift its nose out of the water, breathing in air with its nostrils. It moved through the water by moving its body from side to side, like an eel or a snake. It looks very different from modern whales. When it was first discovered, scientists thought its fossils were those of a giant sea monster!

DID YOU KNOW?

Basilosaurus had a pair of useless back legs. Modern whales have lost the legs, but they still have the hip bones in their skeletons.

Basilosaurus means "Emperor reptile."

Blue Whale

The blue whale is the largest animal to have ever lived. It can grow up to one hundred feet—the length of a jet plane! Its heart is as big as a car, and its tongue is so large that fifty people could stand on it.

Unlike its ancestor, Basilosaurus, the blue whale has **blowholes** instead of nostrils. The blowholes are located at the top of its head. The blue whale also moves its body up and down when it swims, like most marine mammals, instead of side to side like Basilosaurus.

The blue whale can swim at speeds of up to 30 miles an hour.

Instead of teeth, the blue whale has **baleen plates**. These look like combs of very thick hairs. The baleen plates strain krill, which are tiny shrimp-like animals, from the water. To feed, the blue whale dives into the water for ten or twenty minutes, taking as much water as possible into its mouth. Then it forces the water out of its mouth through its baleen plates, trapping the krill inside. Blue whales can eat up to four tons of krill a day!

Unfortunately, due to being hunted almost to extinction in the nineteenth century, the blue whale is currently endangered. But it is being protected, and people around the world are working hard to increase the blue whale population.

DID YOU KNOW?

Tiny krill get caught in the whale's baleen plates when the whale forces water out of its mouth.

Dawn Horse

Many scientists believe that the dawn horse was the first horse. The dawn horse appeared during the Cenozoic era. It was quite small, about the size of a tiny dog! It grew to an average size of two feet long and less than a foot tall.

The dawn horse had four **hoofed** toes on its front feet and three on its back. The bottoms of its toes also had pads, like a dog's toes. This made it easier for the dawn horse to run on the soft ground of the swamps and forests it lived in. It was an herbivore, eating leaves and plants.

DID YOU KNOW?

When the first fossils of the dawn horse were found, their discoverer called the animal a "mole beast."

The dawn horse had 44 teeth.

Zebra

Zebras belong to the same group of animals as horses, donkeys, and their common ancestor, the dawn horse. Every zebra has its own unique pattern of stripes, making it possible to tell individual zebras apart. They live in herds, spending their days wandering around eating grass.

These zebras are enjoying the waterhole.

The zebra's large eyes and ears help it notice predators quickly, so it has a better chance of escaping. Zebras can run up to forty miles an hour, but only for short distances. When a zebra sees a predator, it also makes a loud yelping noise to warn the other zebras!

Megalodon

Megalodon (meg-uh-loh-don), a prehistoric shark that lived during the Cenozoic, was twice as large as today's Great White shark. Its teeth could be up to seven inches long, and it could reach lengths of up to sixty feet and weighed up to fifty tons! Given Megalodon's size, scientists believe it ate mainly whales.

Like modern sharks, Megalodon had **cartilage** instead of bone. Cartilage doesn't make good fossils, so scientists are not sure exactly what Megalodon looked like. They have had to base their ideas of how Megalodon looked and acted on fossils of its teeth.

DID YOU KNOW?

This man is holding a fossil of a modern-day shark's jaw while standing inside a fossil of a Megalodon's jaw!

Great White Shark

Great White sharks are less than half the size of their ancestors, Megalodon, growing only to twenty feet long. They also have a larger diet than Megalodon did, eating smaller sharks, turtles, dolphins, seals, and fish.

Despite what is shown in the movies, Great Whites rarely attack humans. When humans are attacked, it is most likely a case of mistaken identity. The Great White attacks from below, and it may confuse a human's shape in the water with a seal's shape. The Great White doesn't hunt humans, except by accident.

The Great White shark has many rows of teeth, so if a tooth breaks off it is quickly replaced.

Giant Short-Faced Kangaroo

The Giant Short-faced Kangaroo was probably the largest and strangest kangaroo ever. It lived during the Cenozoic era in the forests of Australia. It could grow up to nine feet tall! Though it was slow moving, its powerful back legs allowed it to hop large distances.

This enormous kangaroo had a flat face and hoofed feet like a horse. It had long arms, with two curved claws that looked like hooks on each paw. Unlike modern kangaroos, the Giant Short-faced Kangaroo was able to reach its arms above its head to grab leaves from trees.

The Giant Short-faced Kangaroo became extinct about 50,000 years ago.

Red Kangaroo

The Red Kangaroo is the largest modern-day kangaroo.

Red Kangaroos have shorter bodies and arms than their ancestor, the Giant Short-faced Kangaroo. They are unable to lift their arms above their heads. This may be because they eat mostly grass and don't need to reach tree branches. Their faces aren't nearly as flat as their ancestor's; rather, the Red Kangaroo's face is pointed like a deer's.

Red Kangaroos differ from their ancestor in other ways, too. Red Kangaroos grow to only about five feet, but they have longer tails for balance. They also have four-toed feet, each with a claw that is used for help with jumping. A Red Kangaroo can jump up to thirty feet in just one leap!

Giant Ripper Lizard

The biggest lizard of all time was the giant ripper lizard. It could grow to be twenty feet, and it lived in Australia during the Cenozoic.

The giant ripper lizard had large claws and teeth and could attack and kill animals up to ten times its weight. Scientists think that the giant ripper lizard's mouth had a lot of bacteria in it, so its bite would poison its prey.

The giant ripper lizard could weigh over 1,300 pounds.

Komodo Dragon

The Komodo dragon can have over 50 types of bacteria living in its mouth.

The Komodo dragon is the largest living lizard. It grows to an average of ten feet in length. It has a slimmer body than its ancestor, the giant ripper lizard. The teeth of the Komodo dragon are packed into its mouth more tightly as well.

The Komodo dragon has a poisonous bite like that of its ancestor, the giant ripper lizard. Its mouth is filled with deadly bacteria. People have died from blood poisoning after being bitten by a Komodo dragon!

35

Woolly Mammoth

Scientists believe the woolly mammoth lived in North Africa during the Cenozoic era. Woolly mammoths had the ultimate winter coat—three feet of thick, shaggy hair over a foot of fur and an inner layer of cozy wool. This helped them survive long periods of intense cold.

Wooly mammoths had ten-foot **tusks** that they used to fight other woolly mammoths. They also used these tusks as snow shovels to dig for grass.

Though woolly mammoths were heavier than today's elephants—they weighed around seven tons—they were about the same size.

Woolly mammoths had a layer of fat up to 3 inches thick under their skin to help keep them warm.

Asian Elephant

The Asian elephant grows to about seven to twelve feet tall. Unlike the woolly mammoth, only the male Asian elephant has tusks. The female elephants live in herds, while the males live by themselves.

The Asian elephant uses its trunk for different actions. An elephant drinks by sucking water into its trunk and then squirting the water into its mouth. The tip of its trunk ends in what looks like a small finger, which can be used to grasp things, such as bananas, grass, roots, and leaves.

Asian elephants live for about sixty years.

Animals in the Future

Animals have changed a great deal in the millions of years since the earth first existed. Changes in climate and land led to the extinction of many species of animals. However, many other species of animals have been able to adapt to these changes. Today, the greatest threat most animals face is humans, who hunt animals and use up the land the animals need to survive.

Although we can do nothing about the enormous changes the earth will go through in the future, we can still do something about how many animals become extinct. It is up to us to save as many species as we can, so that they can continue to change with the world around them.

Only around three thousand giant pandas are left in the wild.

Glossary

amphibian a cold-blooded animal, such as a frog, that can live on land and in water and hatches from an egg

arthropod a group of animals, such as insects, spiders, and lobsters, that have a skeleton on the outside of their bodies

baleen plate a plate that strains water and serves as a whale's teeth

blowhole an opening for breathing located at the top of a whale's head

carnivore an animal that eats meat

cartilage a springy tissue that works like a skeleton

efficiently not having to use much effort

endangered close to becoming extinct

extinct no longer existing

fossil animals and plants that have been preserved in rock

geography the study of the earth and its features

herbivore an animal that eats plants

hoofed covered by a hard horn-like material

mammal a warm-blooded animal that makes milk and has live young

mollusk a group of animals that have a soft body and a protective shell

prehistoric before written history

survived remained alive

tusk a long, pointed tooth that extends out of the mouth

wingspan the length from one wingtip to the other